LIGHT UP YOUR LIFE

by **DAVID PHILLIPS**

illustrated by **Mic Rolph**

*Making***sense***of***science**
Children's Books

series editor **Fran Balkwill**

Portland Press

Making sense of science
Children's Books

Other titles in the series

PLANET OCEAN by Brian Bett • **SATELLITE FEVER** by Mike Painter

THE SPACE PLACE by Helen Sharman

We wish to thank the following people who helped in the production of this book:
Editorial Advisor SUSAN DICKINSON
For Portland Press SOPHIE CAYGILL and ADAM MARSHALL
IMPERIAL COLLEGE OF SCIENCE, TECHNOLOGY AND MEDICINE
For supply of spectrum artwork NICK JACKSON, ICSTM

First published in 1997 by Portland Press Ltd
59 Portland Place, London W1N 3AJ, UK

© text David Phillips 1997
© illustrations Mic Rolph 1997

The author asserts the moral right to be identified as the author of the work

ISBN 1 85578 090 9   ISSN 1355 8560

Typeset by Portland Press Ltd
Originated and printed by Cambridge University Press, Cambridge, UK
Hologram produced by Spatial Imaging Ltd, Richmond, UK

All rights reserved. No part of this publication can be reproduced, stored in a retrieval system, or transmitted in any form or by any means, electronic, mechanical, photocopying, recording or otherwise, without the prior permission of the publisher.

Illustration on page 29 inspired by the Pink Floyd album *Pulse*
Illustrations on pages 10 (rod and cone cells) and 16 (volcano) taken from *The Egg and Sperm Race* (1994)
© Text Fran Balkwill illustrations Mic Rolph. Reproduced with permission from
HarperCollins *Publishers* Limited

Light is strange, sometimes dazzling, like sunlight, sometimes dim, like starlight. Light can be coloured, it can be white, it can be invisible. Light zooms at amazing speeds across the Universe. But, most of all, light has incredible power.

Have you ever wondered what light is?

Ummm !..

Scientists think of light as a type of **energy**. Beams of light energy travel as **waves**, or ripples, in straight lines across space. Light waves travel incredibly fast. In fact, they take just one second to travel 300 million metres.

This means that light from the Sun takes only eight minutes to reach us, even though it has to travel 150 million kilometres. Sunlight reflected off the Moon takes just over one second to travel the 400 thousand kilometres to Earth.

We have learnt a great deal about how light behaves and where it comes from, but no one can say exactly what it is.

We do know that life on our planet cannot exist without the energy that comes from light.

Light is a bit like sound. Sound also travels in waves and, like light, it can travel great distances. However, it is much slower. In air, for instance, sound waves travel at only 340 metres per second. When the volcano Krakatoa erupted in Indonesia, it was heard about two hours later by people in Australia thousands of kilometres away. Whales communicate with each other by sending sounds over vast distances in the oceans. Sound waves are also used to find out about the deep-ocean floor. If you were to put your ear to a railway line (don't try it!) you would be able to hear a train coming from several kilometres away. This is because sound has to travel through a substance, such as air, metal, rock or water. Sound cannot travel across a **vacuum**, such as space. You cannot directly hear anything from outer space. All sounds on Planet Earth are contained by its **atmosphere**.

Visible and invisible light energy can travel through a vacuum like space.

This means that you are able to see light from stars billions of kilometres away on the other side of our Galaxy.

With a powerful telescope you can see light that has travelled for millions of years from stars in other galaxies.

You **see** in a **universe of light**.

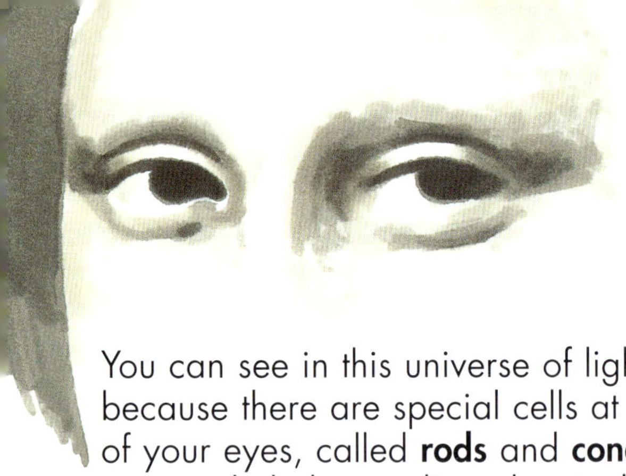

You can see in this universe of light because there are special cells at the back of your eyes, called **rods** and **cones**. They react to light by sending electrical signals to your brain. But the rod and cone cells recognize only a tiny fraction of all of the light energy. You are able to see only **red**, **orange**, **yellow**, **green**, **blue**, **indigo** and **violet** light. The rest of the light energy in the Universe is invisible to human eyes.

You see all colours mixed together as white light. You can prove this by shining white light through a **prism** and seeing it split into different colours. A rainbow is created when white light from the Sun is split by millions of raindrops.

To make all possible shades of colour, you need just a red light, a green light and a blue light. Colour televisions use the same three colours. By mixing them in many different combinations, all the colours of our world can be made. This sort of light is called **emitted** light.

You can also see colour as **reflected** light. Imagine you are in a green field, dressed in blue, and looking at red flowers. The things you see are not emitting green, blue and red light waves. You see these colours because your clothes, the grass and the flowers have **absorbed** some of the other visible light waves. When white light shines on a red flower, chemicals called **pigments** absorb all the blue and green light. The flower looks red because it reflects red light into your eyes. Grass looks green because it has a pigment that absorbs red and blue light. It reflects only green light. What colour light waves have been absorbed by your blue clothes?

If you mix red, green and blue paints, what colour do you think you will get? Why don't you try it? It certainly won't be the same colour as you would get from mixing red, green and blue light, which would give you white light. Mixing the paints would make a blackish colour. The mixture looks black because the paints absorb nearly all the colours of the rainbow and no light is reflected into your eyes.

Scientists think that light waves are made of streams of **photons**. Photons are particles of light energy. Photons that make up the different forms of light have different energies and make different waves. The higher the energy, the shorter the distance between the peaks of these waves. This distance is called the **wavelength**.

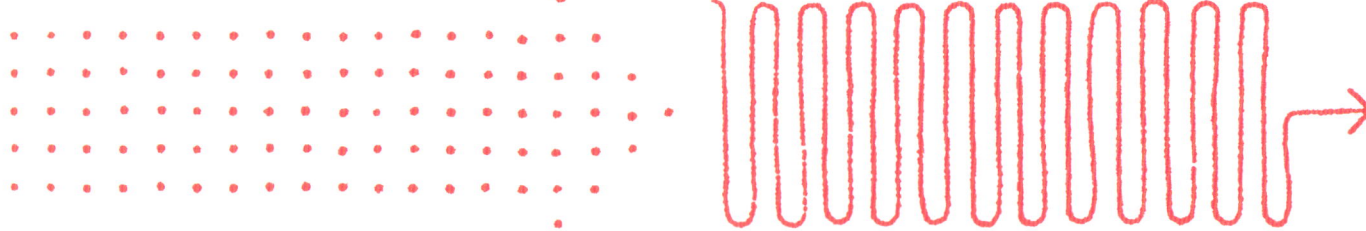

Radio waves are one type of invisible light. They have the weakest energy. A ray one metre long would contain less than one-thousandth of a single wave. A typical radio wave is about one kilometre long.

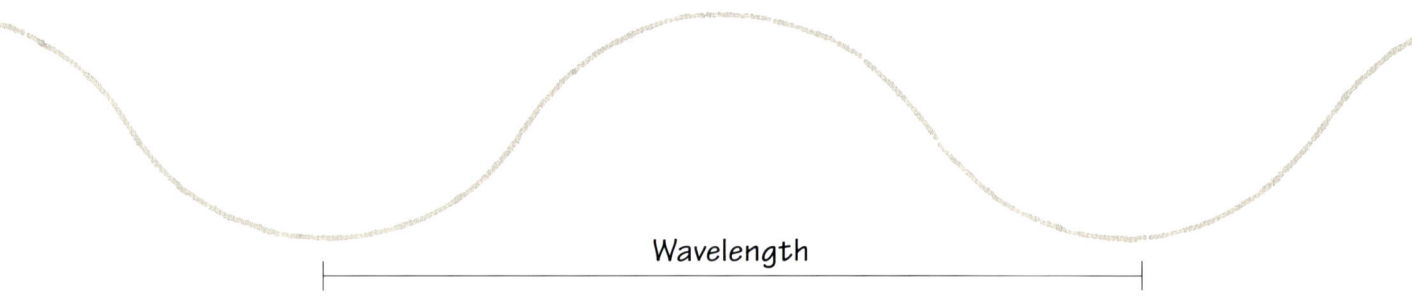

Visible red light has a lot more energy. A ray of red light just one metre long would contain about one and a half million waves.

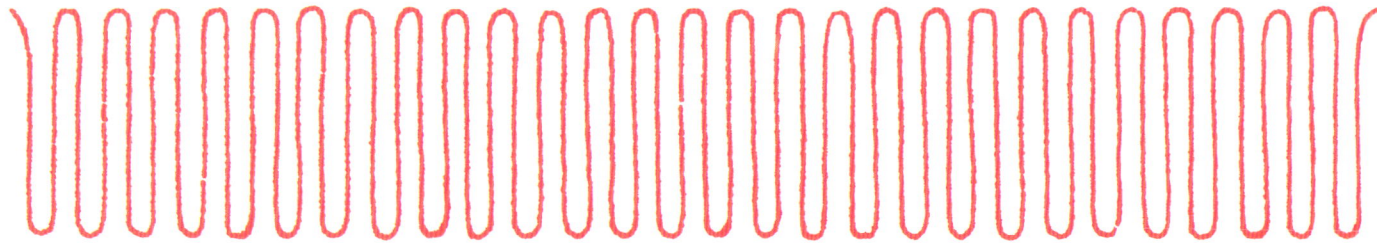

A one metre long ray of pure blue light has even more energy. It would be made of a total of two and a half million waves.

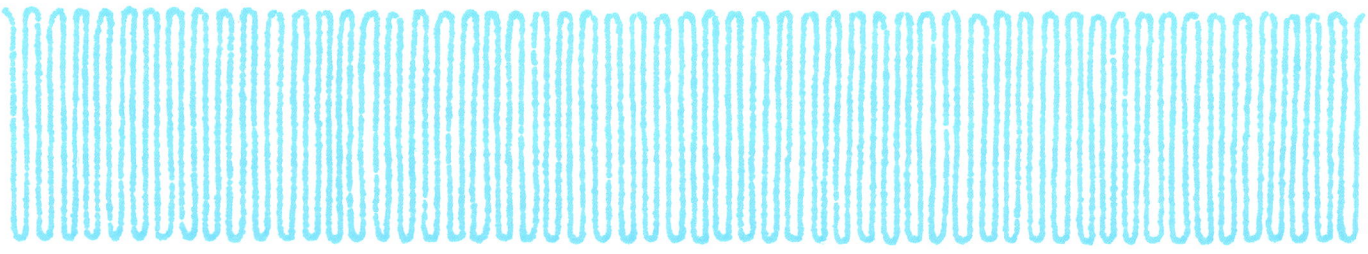

X-rays are a type of invisible light made of photons of very high energy. A one metre long beam of X-rays would be made of ten thousand million waves.

There is another name for all these visible and invisible light rays. They are called **electromagnetic waves** and together they make up the **electromagnetic spectrum**.

Here's a little wave of my own !

Planet Earth is continually being bombarded with light energy.

Radio waves are invisible light waves with the weakest energy.

They carry signals from transmitters on aerials and satellites to radios or televisions, so that you can listen to music and watch your favourite programmes.

Microwaves are invisible light waves used for sending telephone, television and radar signals.

They can also cook and heat food very quickly. A beam of microwaves penetrates the food. Water in the food absorbs energy from the waves and gets hot, thus heating the food.

Infra-red waves are simply heat waves that come from warm and hot objects. Infra-red light makes you feel warm by transferring energy to your body. Some snakes can 'see' infra-red. This is extremely handy for catching their prey. Even in the dark, they can detect heat from their victim's body.

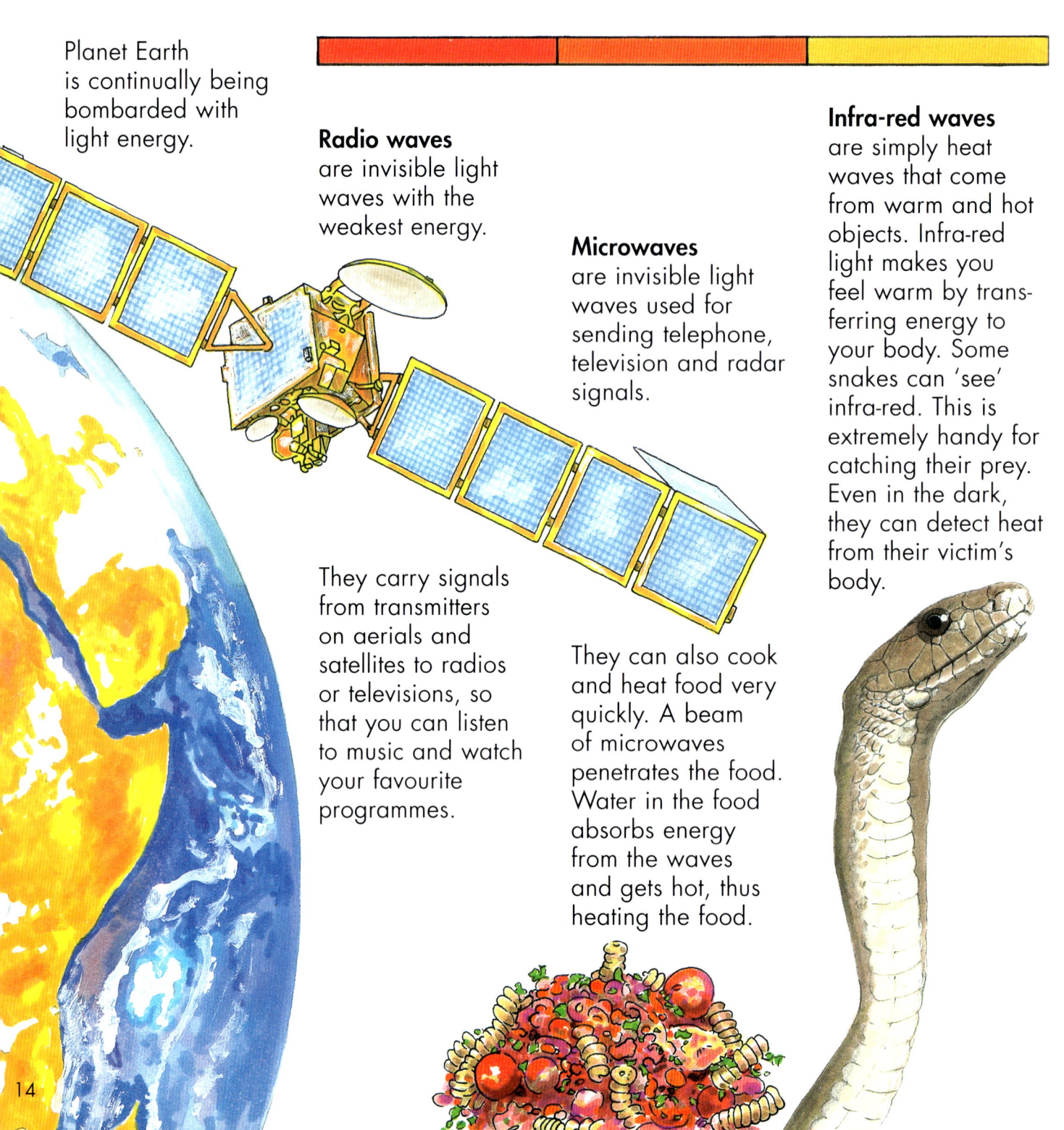

Visible light waves are red, orange, yellow, green, blue, indigo and violet. They are the only part of the electromagnetic spectrum that human eyes can see.

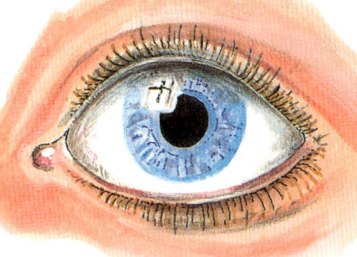

Ultraviolet waves come from the Sun and from some fluorescent lamps. Ultraviolet light is higher in energy than violet light. It transfers energy to your skin cells, they produce more pigment and you become suntanned (or burnt, which can be dangerous). Some insects can see ultraviolet. White flowers all look the same colour to us, but ultraviolet patterns on different flowers help butterflies to distinguish between them.

X-rays have more energy. Using a special photographic plate, doctors use X-rays to 'see' the hard bits of your body. X-rays travel through all the soft bits and darken a photographic plate, but they cannot penetrate hard bits, like bones. Bones are seen as white images on the dark background.

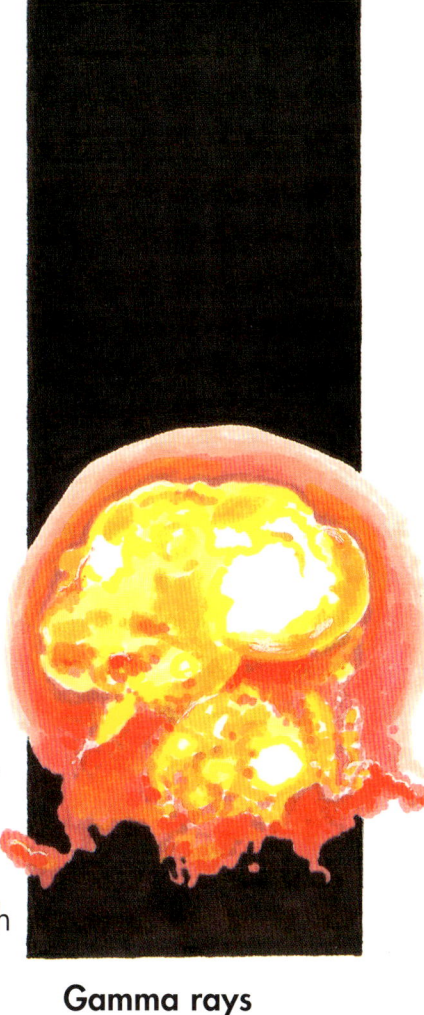

Gamma rays have the highest energy of all and come from radioactive substances and nuclear reactions. **They can be lethal!**

When Planet Earth was first formed, its light came from the Sun and stars, or from lightning flashes in the sky. Five billion years later, most of the light on our planet still comes from the Sun. The Sun is hot, 6000 °C on the outside (and much hotter at the core). Something that gives out light when it is heated is **incandescent** (in-can-dess-ent).

Some light on Earth is made by chemical reactions called **chemiluminescence** [deep breath...] (kem-ee-loom-in-ess-ence). This light is much weaker than sunlight. Bacteria, fungi and some animals have evolved to make light in this way. Have you ever seen glow-worms or fire-flies at night?

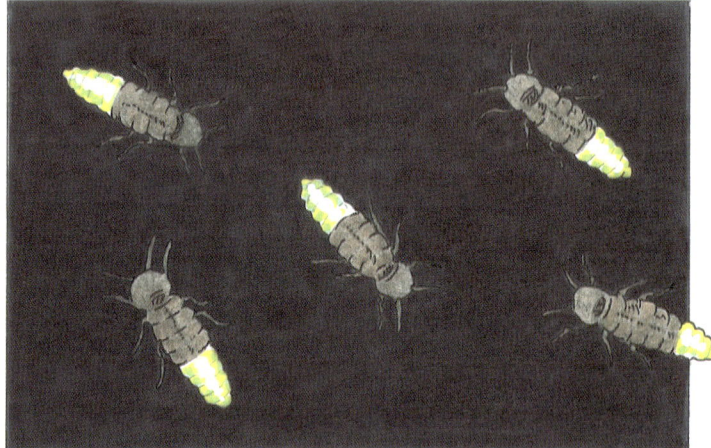

Because there is no light in the deep sea, some animals have developed a unique way of catching their prey. For instance, millions of years ago the angler fish had a light-making spot on its head. This probably wasn't much use. The fish evolved so that the light was at the end of a slender tube that dangled right in front of its mouth.

The light makes small animals very curious...

Early humans quickly learned to harness the power of light with a most important discovery, fire. Fire gave them not only light, but also warmth, during the long, dark nights of the Ice Age.

All over the world, scientists and inventors have found many different ways to make light. Burning is still used to provide light from fireworks, coal fires, oil lamps, matches and candles.

Light bulbs powered by electricity or batteries have a hot wire, incandescent filament. Domestic gas is also burnt to give light and heat. **Neon** lights make red light by passing a very small electrical current through a gas. **Argon** lights are blue in colour. In a **fluorescent** (floor-ess-ent) tube-light, weak light from the gas is made stronger by a special coating on the tube that gives out a strong white light.

Light is also made by passing a small electric current through a special solid, a **light-emitting diode** or **LED**. This is the light you see on a music centre, car dashboard and television control panel. Light sticks and glowing necklaces, which you find in funfairs, make light by chemiluminescence.

I've seen the light!

The most amazing way that scientists have ever discovered to make light is a **laser**.

The word laser comes from the first letters of five words.

Light (you should know what that is by now)

Amplification (making the light brighter)

by **S**timulated (forcing it)

Emission (to be given out)

of **R**adiation (really just another word for light)

Lasers harness the fantastic energy of light. They give us the most powerful 'man-made' source of light energy on the planet.

Once you understand a little about light, it is not that difficult to make a laser, although the first one was not made until recently, in 1960. How do lasers work?

First you need a structure to house the laser. Then you need a substance that is very good at emitting light when hit by a source of energy. It can be gas, liquid or solid. This substance is called the **medium**.

To make a laser, you need to 'excite' the basic building blocks of the medium, the **atoms** and **molecules**. This can be done with a charge of electricity, by light or by chemical reactions.

Next you need two mirrors, one at each end of the laser housing. The first mirror, at the back, reflects all the light that is made. The other, at the front, lets a little of the light through. This makes the **laser beam**.

A laser beam looks like a straight, almost solid, rod of intense light.

Let's see what happens inside a laser...

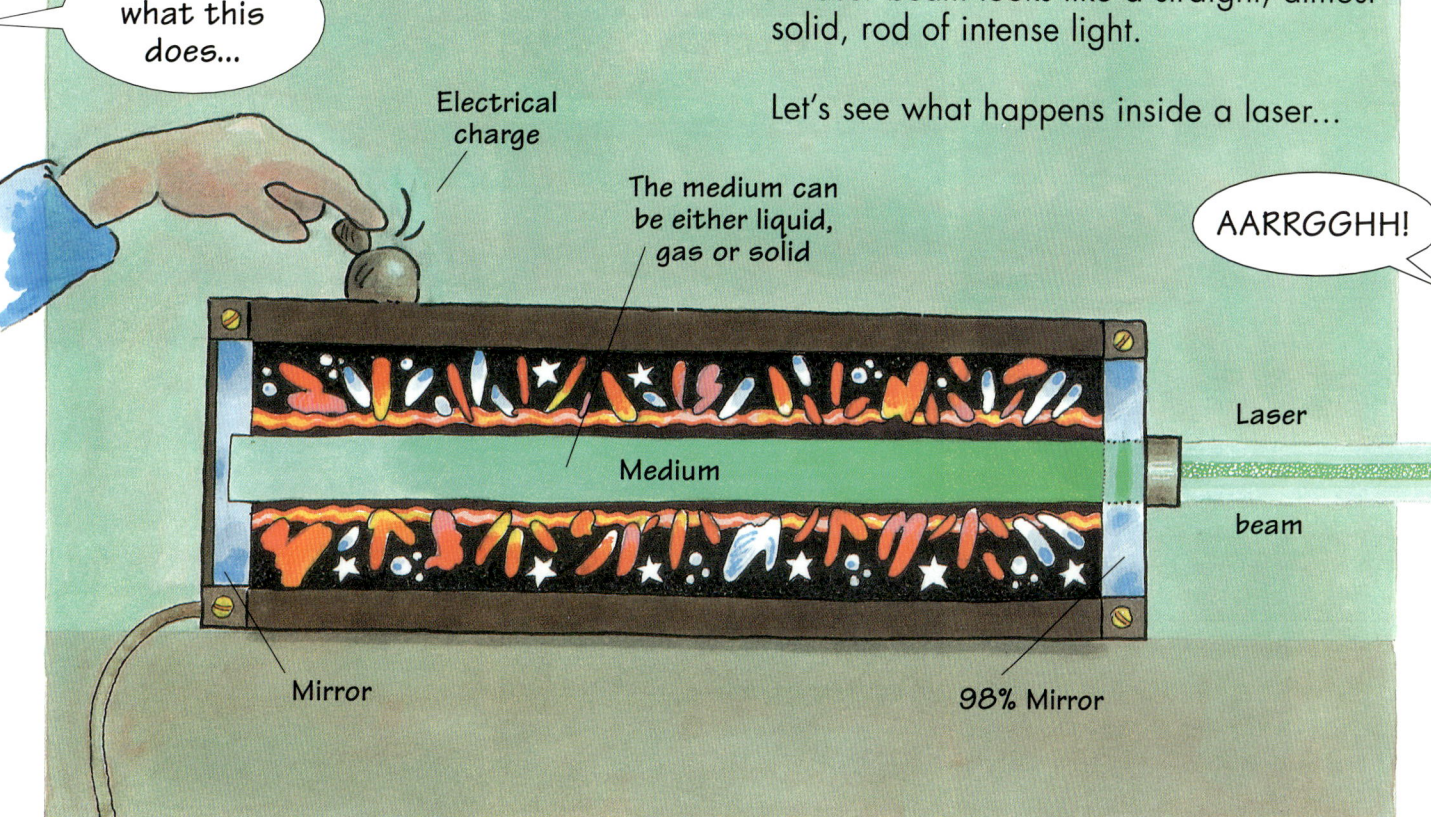

We will start with a single atom in the laser medium.

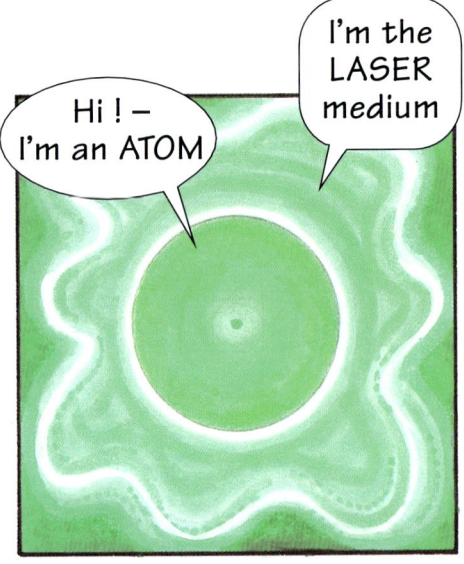

An atom is the smallest single particle of an element. It has a centre, called a **nucleus**, and **electrons** which move in orbits around its centre.

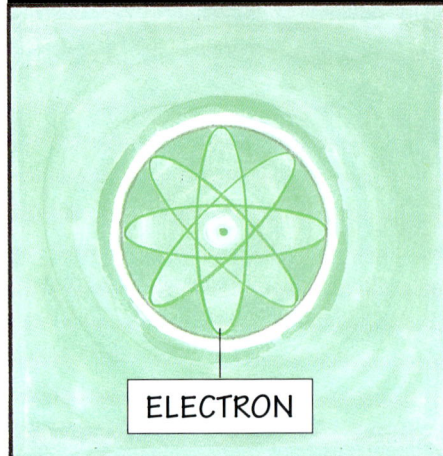

When the atom absorbs light energy, an electron jumps to an orbit further away from the nucleus. This is the way the atom stores light energy.

The excited atom cannot stay in a high-energy state for long. The electron drops back to its original orbit and gives out a photon of light. This is called **emission**.

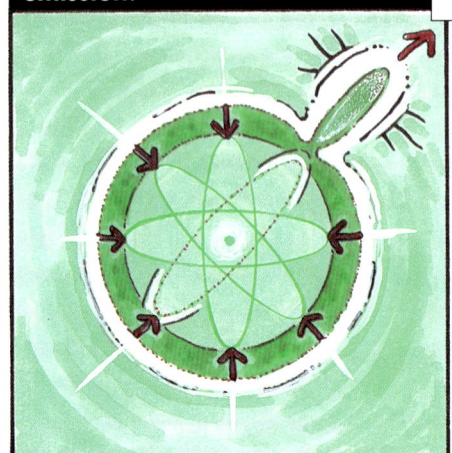

When it happens naturally, and only a few atoms are excited in the medium, it is called **spontaneous** emission.

But if a photon meets an atom that is already excited, it forces or **stimulates** that atom to give out a photon, like the first one. Now there are two photons.

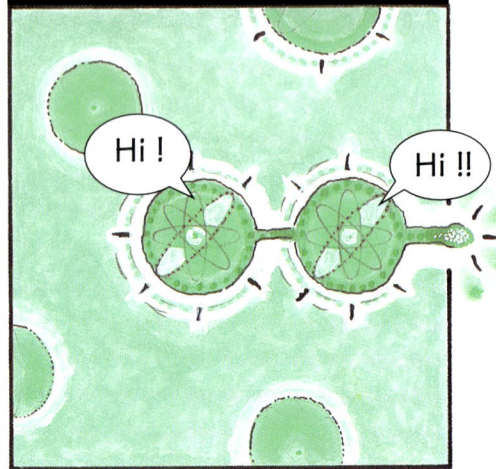

If these two photons hit two more excited atoms, four photons will be given out.

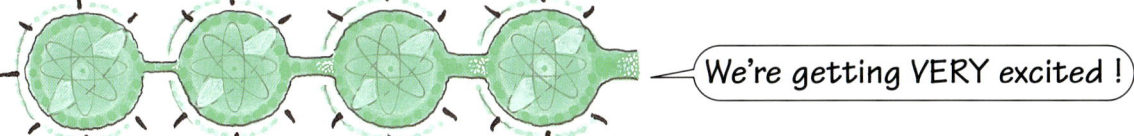

When those four photons hit four excited atoms, eight photons are released. At the next stage, sixteen photons are released, and so it goes on. This is the **amplification** stage.

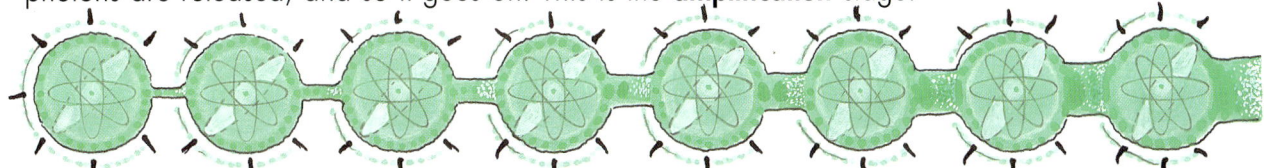

All this is not enough to make a laser unless the medium is hit by a very powerful source of energy, so that more than half of its billions of atoms become excited at about the same time.

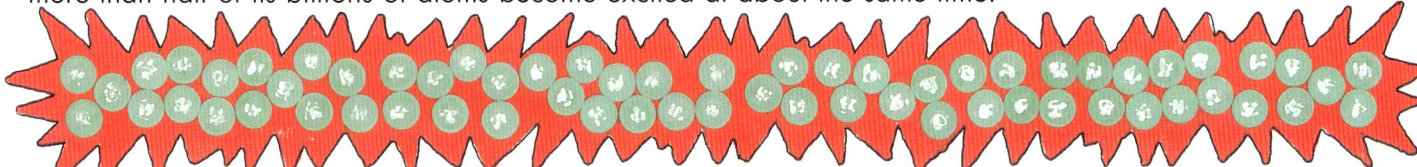

Soon the medium starts 'lasing'. Photons bounce into one excited atom after another. All the time the light intensity is becoming more powerful.

Light bounces back and forth between the mirrors, getting brighter and brighter as atoms are stimulated to emit...

...until a bright, high-energy laser light (**radiation**) shines in a thin, sparkling line from the front mirror.

Light waves from an ordinary light source are all muddled up. The waves spread out in all directions so that the light quickly fades. The light from a laser is like one giant wave. It is called a **coherent** (coe-here-rent) light source. All the atoms emit light at the same time. Like soldiers marching in step, the light waves are all travelling in a straight line and in the same direction. They are of identical length and identical colour. Light from a laser is a narrow shaft of very intense bright light. This beam stays together over huge distances, even from the Earth to the Moon or beyond!

The LASER is fired at the moon....
Do you remember how long the beam would take to get there?

The light source (or medium) of a laser can be made from liquids, solids and gases. Lasers are made from substances as diverse as liquid dyes, precious stones such as rubies, or gases like helium, neon, nitrogen or argon. The light that they make can be any colour of the spectrum, or invisible, for example infra-red, or even ultraviolet.

You should not be able to see a laser beam. None of the light will enter your eyes unless you look directly at its source, which could be extremely dangerous. However, you can see a beam because dust in the air blocks some of the waves. This scatters a small amount of the beam into your eyes, and you see a dazzlingly bright, twinkling ray of light.

When the first lasers were made, there were few obvious uses for them. In fact, they were 'a solution in search of a problem'! Now lasers are used in almost every part of human life on the planet...

If you split a laser beam in two, and send one beam to a photographic plate while the other reflects off an object onto the same photographic plate, the two waves interfere. (It is a bit like throwing two stones into a pond and watching what happens when the two sets of ripples spread out. In some places the waves disappear, in others there is a bigger wave.) In the case of the light reaching the photographic plate, sometimes a brighter light results, and the plate darkens. Sometimes the two waves cancel out, there is no light, and the plate does not darken. The pattern produced on the plate is called a **hologram**.

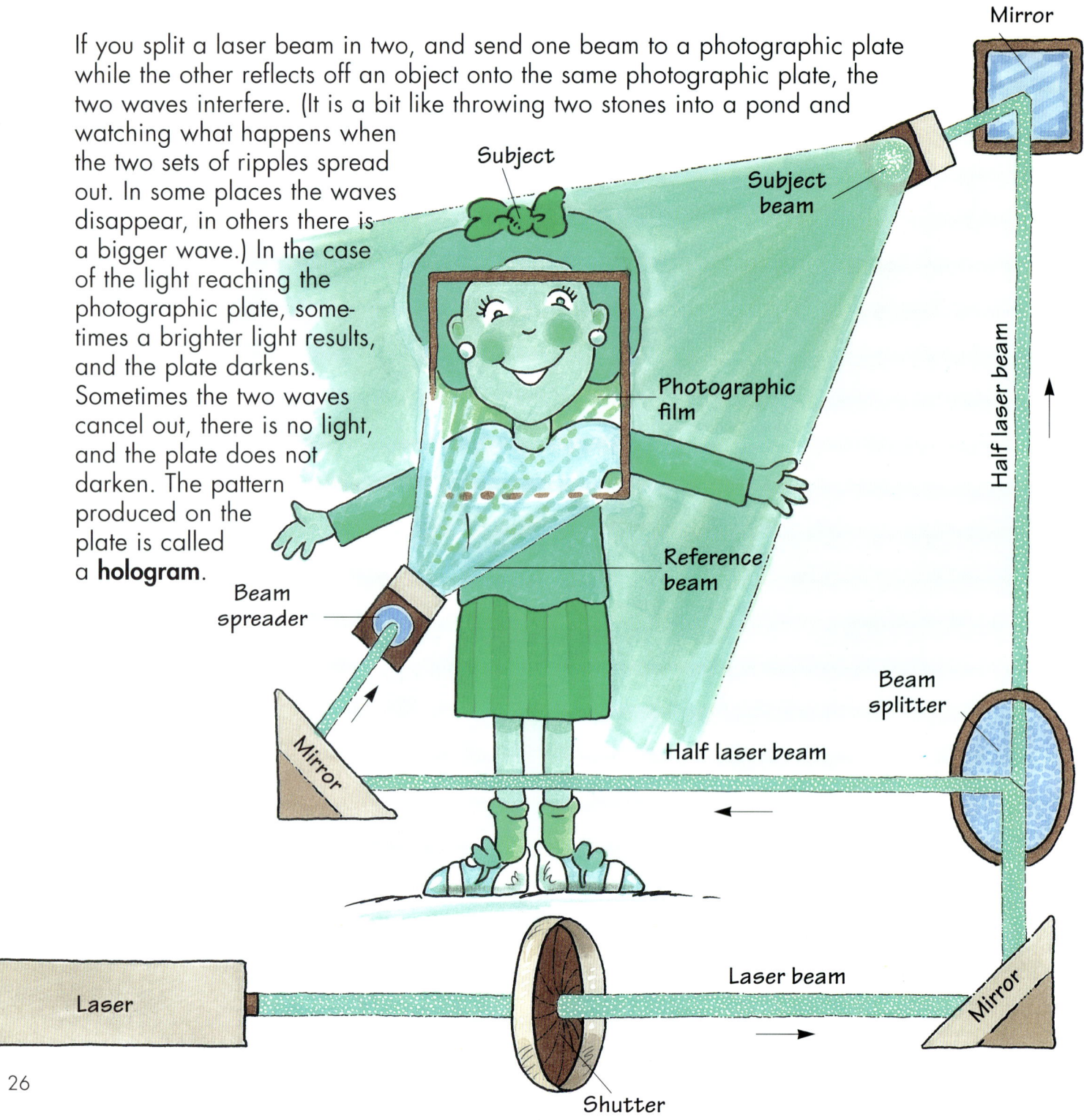

To see a hologram, you need to shine light of the same colour used to produce it onto the plate. What is astonishing about a hologram is that the image is three-dimensional (3-D), just like the original object.

There is a real hologram on the back of this book.

Few people have lasers at home for viewing holograms, so a way has been found to see them in white light. A coating is used on the hologram which absorbs most of the light and only lets through light of the same colour as the original laser. If you look at a hologram at a different angle, the right colour of light is reflected from a bit lower down. This means you can store many holograms at different depths and, by moving your head slightly (or the hologram), you can see the picture moving.

It will not be long before you will be able to watch moving holograms on 3-D television or films at the cinema.

If you looked at a **compact disc** (CD) under a microscope, you would see it has lots of little 'pits' (like shallow holes) in it. These are made when the disc is pressed, and, if you could 'read' it, you would discover it has **digital information**, as in a computer. You can turn music or speech into digital form and store it on a CD, but when you want to hear it, you have to be able to read it. This is done for you in your CD player by a small **diode laser**, which is focused on the disc, which moves around as it is read. The laser sees either a hole, or no hole. This is digital information. The CD player turns these signals back into music or speech, which you can hear.

Video discs work in the same way, and so do CD-ROMs, which are able to store a huge amount of information on one CD. At the moment, the limit to the amount of information stored is the wavelength of the light, usually infra-red or red. The shorter the wavelength, the tighter the light can be focused, and the smaller the pits which can be seen and read. If we could use blue or ultraviolet lasers to read discs, we could store much more music or text. This might soon be possible, but you will have to buy a brand new CD player!

In laser light shows, the light from visible lasers is steered by moving mirrors. The light beams are made to move or pulse in time to the music. The effects can be very dramatic. If the light is projected on to a screen, moving images are made.

If you have ever been to a laser light show, you might have noticed that there was a lot of artificial smoke in the air. The laser beams would be invisible, unless some of their light was reflected off dust or the chemical smoke into your eyes. With the smoke, you can see the laser light pulsing with the music.

Scientists and engineers are designing military lasers that will be able to attack dangerous enemy missiles high above Earth. These awesome laser weapons can be placed inside a jumbo-jet, for instance. The dust in the atmosphere can scatter the deadly beams, but computer-controlled mirrors adjust their shape thousands of times per second, so the beam is always focused on its target. In tests, these airborne chemical lasers were able to hit and destroy Cruise missiles. The plan is that they could hover over war zones and shoot down missiles far away from the

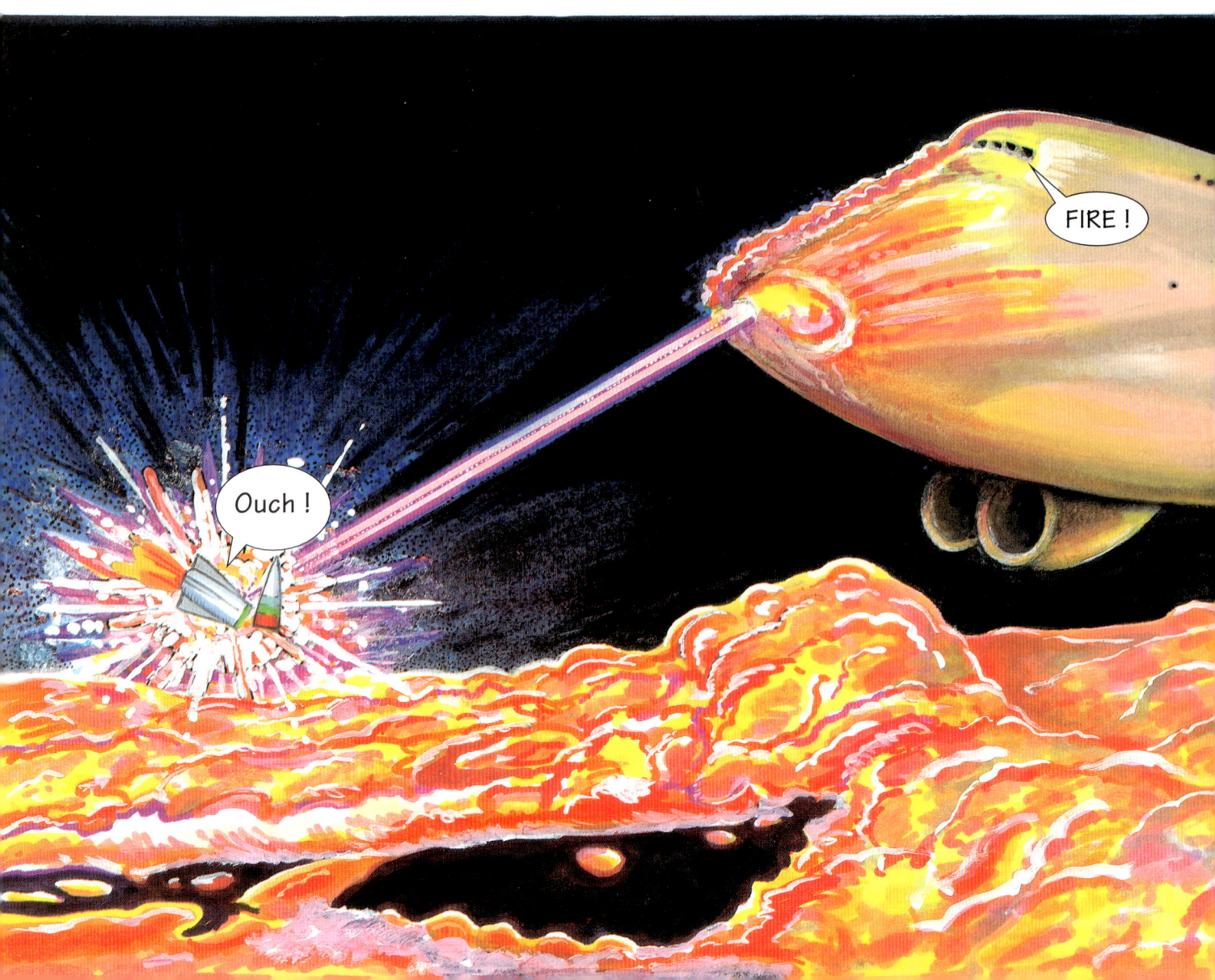

Earth's surface, hopefully causing much less damage than they would on Earth. It would be best, however, for these lasers to be outside the Earth's atmosphere. Here there is no dust, so the light would not scatter at all. Laser weapons could be mounted on **satellites** orbiting deep in space.

A radio signal from Earth would release an accurate ray of destructive light to blast enemy missiles... or even an unfriendly spaceship from a distant galaxy!

Scientists have made lasers that are frighteningly powerful
— many billions of times stronger than a single light bulb.

There is so much energy in these lasers that they can turn any material into a hot gas, called a **plasma**. If hydrogen is used as the material, you get a **hydrogen plasma**, which is exactly what the Sun is.

Using lasers, scientists have made hydrogen plasmas in the laboratory that are almost as hot as the inside of the Sun. When the plasma reaches a very hot state, it behaves like the Sun and starts **thermonuclear** (therm-oh-new-clee-ah) reactions, which emit huge amounts of energy.

We might soon be able to make limitless energy on Earth from these mini-suns.

Then lasers would really

LIGHT UP YOUR LIFE